W9-BGM-786

Praise for #Dear Twitter:

@mobrowne u inspire my fearlessness & enable my growth. what a galactic force of nature you are, proof that the universe continues to amaze.
@aja_monet

I follow @mobrowne for the effortless way she reflects upon & speaks to life in (give or take) 140 characters. Her letters are the definition of "retweetability."
@ShanelleG

@mobrowne's letters pull the ether into your internet. she sends wishes well, offers up a hallelujah that you can finally reply to.
@PonyJones

@mobrowne somewhere there's a woman in Detroit reading your tweets, thinking about your knowledge and saying: God gave us black girls.
@tmillerpoetry

dear @twitter, whether it's in gentle musing, stern admonition, or everyday sweetness, when @mobrowne calls you dear, honey; pay attention.
@londyjamel

Dear @mobrowne, your tweets make me want to be in love, live in Brooklyn, be a better poet, slap stupid people & then buy them coffee.
@tavisbrunson

Some people just know how to fit the corners of the universe into 140 characters. That's genius. Aka @mobrowne.
@KamoneFromPluto

@mobrowne's tweets: (noun) plu. : a combination of real talk, tough love, and poetic justice dressed in pink ribbons & shark's teeth. See also: modern feminism, the politics of art, social trailblazers, truth for the masses.
@phoenixpoet

@mobrowne your tweets are therapuetic and inspirational, if you ever stop then twitter will have lost one of their most useful assets.
@bonafiderojas

@mobrowne mahogany browne is the reason I downloaded the twitter app. All day.
@megan_falley

#DEAR TWITTER:
LOVE LETTERS HASHED OUT ONLINE IN 140 CHARACTERS OR LESS

BY MAHOGANY L. BROWNE

a **penmanship** book

Published by Penmanship Publishing Group
593 Vanderbilt Avenue, #265
Brooklyn, NY 11238

Copyright © 2010 by Mahogany L. Browne
Book Design by A. J. Stabe
Author Photo by Jose Infante

All rights reserved. This book may not be reproduced in
whole or in part (except in the case of reviews) without
written permission from author.

First Penmanship trade edition: September 2010

To contact Mahogany L. Browne please visit
www.penmanshipbooks.com

ISBN # 978-0-09841513-9-4
Printed in The United States of America

mobrowne

#dear twitter is my homage to the beautiful and lost art of writing letters. i wanted to have fun and really dissect the everyday thing. like the importance of a kiss, of telling yourself that you are worthy, of reminding your bones that love is everywhere…the bodega, the slice of lemon cake, the single woman's shoulder, the new kiss, the friends that hold you tight, the light that holds you accountable, the city streets that blink alive in the wake of our footsteps.

#dear twitter: is a handful of loveletters to you.

#dear self: this is the big one. Practice breathing. Leave your hands to floating—don't thrash, even when the small fish get in the way.

#dear self: most people are not built for your journey, don't blame them for their lack of commitment. Nor yourself for believing in them.

#dear right: you dead wrong

#dear self: the house is a movable thing, your faith is not.

#dear self: the earth is a shakeable thing, your integrity is not.

#dear daughter: i fear for ur safety. i pray for the way u rise like the sun. i praise the day u see all this fight in my marrow is 4 u

#dear she: the trend is to follow your heart, not your friends.

#dear hater: you make me smile. you got the cutest sneer in the world

#dear hip hop: I want all our children to feel beautiful for being who they are…

#dear you, a haiku: "if he wasn't shyt/ when you fukd him trust me/ he aint shyt after"

#dear lover: there is something about you that makes even the snoring sound like a loving lullaby. when its just allergies and dehydration.

#dear beautiful wonderous man: poems reside in your spine, i trace them lovely while you sleep, lie still…

#dear she: he is never worth your sanity. Never worth the parts of you charred in the fire sale.

#dear heart: the way you spill and burst and twist into this puddle. you are of the messiest sorts. its the part i love about you most.

#dear swag: i know haters never prosper. That's why I'm nap this one off. "In Swag I Trust"

#dear you: I'm always at a loss of words at the idea of losing you.

#dear you: its easier 2stand w/the crowd in silence than speak ur truth 2 the wind. it is also less satisfying. u didnt come this far 4 less

#dear self: any man that loves your stretchmarks the way he loves your smile is a keeper

#dear husband to be: you ask me to marry you—we're tying the knot like, yesterday

#dear internet thug: you are the epitome of corny. what are you going to do—beat me to death with your shift button?

#dear self: there is a poem waiting for you on the other side of this pain.

#dear skinny chicks: i am not a hater if i wanna stuff a coupla' donuts in ya face. im all about equality. ur metabolisticness is just unfair

#dear he: thats unafraid of romance. it is the little things u know. the elbow hold & patient glance. those are what makes fairytales boring

#dear heavy heart: it was just a dream. and you deserve dreams with happy endings, believe that.

#dear bones: u will break. dear spirit: u will shatter. dear heart: u will bruise again & again, but u will be the hardest to fix w/o faith

#dear lover: the way you speak to my skin is melodic. sing it this way every day. the sun ain't got nuthin on your shine.

#dear you: i dreamt of u w/whiskey on my breath and song in my spine and no obvious reason to wake up and say i love except for this—i do

#dear you: my skin is lonely. Bring me ur weight, ur worry, ur doubt. Let it keep me company.

#dear heart: try not to skip a beat. try not to stumble and break into bits and pieces of why?

#dear him: to he who is not ready to love me. leave now, your freedom is all you've got. and my sanity is important to me.

#dear love: u feel like home. this is the reason I fear the threat
of your daunting kiss

#dear world: i be worth it. act accordingly.

#dear biters: i used to worry about what you was doing, second
hand wearing my swag. but now i see—you just playing
dress up.

#dear sista: any woman that would toss their pussy to the wind
& a knife into another woman's back is not worth the beatdown
she deserves.

#dear Facebook: ur so selfish. The way u break up families. All
that single/complicated crap. U nurture the stalker tendencies
in us all.

#dear world: i went to sleep doubting this shade and woke up
back in love with myself.

DEAR YOU: OUR SWAG BE THE BRILLIANCE SUNS ARE MADE OF

#dear moon: if you had arms, i can only imagine…

#dear moon: you be splitting the backs open with them crater sized dimples. imma need you to show me how to smile like that.

#dear everything i love: show yourself. i need you now. more than ever.

#dear hater: thank you for the energy. i was tired and near giving up. then you and your hater face appear and i know—its gonna be alright

#dear donny hathaway: sing me unbroken, again

#dear nina simone: sing me beautiful, again and again

#dear dearest: my chest hurts, i suspect this is how my heart runs after the one she loves…

#dear he unafraid to love me: you are brave and miraculous man. i will treat you accordingly.

#dear she: no one can take from you what you haven't already given them.

#dear self: never settle for anything that squeezes your spine like a rubber band.

#dear good: what's god?

#dear allergies: your momma.

#dear swag: you are a burden, yet a beautiful beast

#dear black: you've got to win the war in your head before you attempt to fight the war against your skin

#dear self: you are a worthwhile

#dear world: i got this brown eyed bombshell. she thinks like a grenade and sings like a missile. watch your step.

#dear twitter: i can't be foolin' with you all night. youre like the boyfriend thats super needy with little return.

#dear self: pamper yourself. w/each accomplishment serve yourself a gift. w/each failure, present yourself w/the opportunity to try again.

#dear daughter: repeat after me.

#dear Brooklyn: i walked your flatbush spine like a cat walk.

#dear twitter: all hair is good hair.

#dear twitter: but all weave, is unfortunately not, good weave.

#dear daughter: any man that promises to love you like an oil spill; slick and consumptuous, think twice before testing the waters.

#dear self: the only thing you can trust is the breaking of your bones. one day even your breath will leave you.

DEAR SMILE:

you are SUN

a wonderful SUN

you are SUN

a wonderful SUN

you are

you are

the dust will rise and fall in your wake

#dear you: i dont like to give directions all the time. sometimes a lady just wants u to know how to pull the heartstrings w/out the manual

#dear procrastination: you make it so easy to forget i had something to do

#dear self: fall in love with you again. rise in love with tomorrow.

#dear you: I wish your flaws were as beautiful as I wrote them. But they're not. They're human. And that's ok, too.

#dear diet: you're dumb. Even when u work. Ur still dumb.

#dear he: I am worth all of it. Are you?

#dear poems: fly out my spine, create a whirlwind of my bones, tear my wings into flight.

#dear self: there is a bomb in your chest and pocketful of regrets. but you have survived.

#dear tonguetied man: I think its sweet. That grown men still find a shadow to hold tight their tongue. To surrender to the moment of blush.

#dear self: when u bite ur tongue—its your own blood u taste, not heaven.

#dear she: your p*ssy is not #unfukwitable, your spirit is.

#dear he: if you lie between a woman's legs make sure she is who you prayed for, anything less is a sin against your own holy.

#dear self: anyone that holds you when you cry is a firm yes. an amen. and a hallelujah.

#dear he: your smile is my kryptonite. do it often. please.

#dear self: you are the moon. The lovely sky is always star speckled envious of you

#dear self: romance is not just for movies. its for a heart like yours.

#dear self: declare your love for you. for safety. for home. for stay. for him. for her. for us. for now. for now. for more than now. amen

#dear self: ur beauty be in the mistakes, like when u fell in love w/a man that didnt deserve u & rose out the ashes in love with urself

DEAR TWITTER:

SLEEP IS OVERRATED.

NOW EATING, EATING IS THE SHYT.

SO IS LOVE.

BUT YOU CAN'T EAT LOVE...

#dear self: playing dumb, is dumb. playing smart is
awesome sauce

#dear self: lie next to the body that curves best with yours.

#dear self, the power of no is yours. practice it.

#dear octupus heart woman: you got 3 hearts, 8 legs and a
mouth of many talents.

#dear he: i could be in love with you, especially when you talk
politics, hip hop, evolution, poetry—especially when you
allow me in.

#dear self: the day you look betrayal in the eye is when you
fall in love with another person more than yourself.

#dear self: u found yourself in hip hop, in his acceptance, in their applause but the day u found yourself in your own reflection was magic.

#dear hip hop: i often wonder if you are god. i reckon you could be her

#dear she: have you ever smelled your spirit on its best day? it dont smell like p*ssy or money or man. it smell like freedom.

#dear self: fall upwards

#dear Brooklyn: i want to buy a house in ur belly. i want my family to visit & rest well & know the sound of ur laughter

#dear poet: poems are edible, when they're written the right way

#dear twitter its still a black thing. sometimes i dont even understand

#dear self: the air catches its breath when it sees you.

#dear twitter: i try not to check his facebook and decode the women's post. hearts and smiley face?

#dear twitter: the first woman i ever fell in love with was my mother. we should all know a bliss like this.

#dear twitter: my poetry isnt for everyone. like sonia sanchez, i write so i dont have to kill nobody.

#dear heart: you break like a banshee, dont let them cage you

DEAR   SELF:

YOU BE IN LOVE

LIKE MOST DARE

TO DREAM. THIS

IS A GIFT. TO

LIVE WITH YOUR

CHEST   OPEN

WIDE, LIKE THAT

#dear twitter: i have a problem with people and bad breath. no hugging. only fist dap for you, homie.

#dear twitter: ive got stretchmarks, bumps, bruises & the scar from the ankle surgery…but i still walk around this piece like im airbrushed

#dear twitter: i watch people kiss. i love PDA. ive had rare dances with it myself. But I think its some type of wonderful

#dear universe: give me the gift of the nighttime, a shadow and his mouth.

#dear him: i don't have a lot of time. but i got a lot of heart, it is yours.

#dear twitter: no one goin' love me like i love me. this is what i say to myself in the mirror

#dear self: you are the only you that matters

#dear twitter: the bravest thing you can ever do is open your
entire chest to someone else

#dear self: everyone got a spine—but not all of them got the
know-how for heartholding.

#dear self: you are done when you are done and no one knows
your limit but you.

#dear self: ur heart is the more beautiful than your greatest
accomplishment. dont be afraid of its power to bruise and heal
and grow bigger

#dear him: to he who is not ready to love me. leave now, your
freedom is all you've got. and my sanity is important to me.

DEAR
SHE:
WE BE
FALLING SHORT
OF OUR OWN
EXPECTATIONS
CAUSE WE
TOO BUSY
TRYNNA
CREATE MEN
FROM THE
SHARDS
OF THEIR
SHORTCOMINGS

#dear love: it is you that makes the day worth waking up to. the idea of you of sharing you with someone thats worthy spins me silly.

#dear sir: I won't leave bruises, ignore ur strength, deny ur dream or bring u pain if u promise to offer me the same.

#dear self: do not mistake loyalty for love.

#dear Brooklyn: u look beautiful today. Thank u for that.

#dear young'n: we signifies all of us. There are no stupid questions—but ur the exception.

#dear NYC: u made this cali girl anti-social. I've learned so much from u. NO: staring, touching, talking to or smiling @ strangers

#dear self: the most beautifullest thing in this world is ur smile. Show it, often.

#dear friend: my punches are only a flurry of truth. i will never hurt you intentionally.

#dear lover: he who brings me tea when my pain is heavier than my hope, is the man that will know my thankful smile is a promised whisper

#dear unoriginal artist: please stray from becoming a field of mines detonating only when touched.

#dear us: memories are heavy. in this case. not too heavy for a spoon of cherry vanilla ice cream.

#dear lover: thank u 4 appreciating the complexity. the break & bend of my back. the reinforced spirit the gasping bright & pretty heart

dear diet: we goin' have to make a deal. i'm
going to have my first order of french toast
and you're going to look the other way.
boom

#dear she: u r the reason i write @ all i will continue 2write our song until we all know the words beautiful necessary worthy holy by heart

#dear hottentot venus: i can only imagine your disdain. we are sorry. all of us. we know not what we do with this silence.

#dear booty pop (panties w/but implants sewn in): you are a world of ridiculous.

#dear she: imma need you to take responsibility. there are some of us that should be held accountable for breaking the spirit of good men.

#dear she: the fear that fills our womb at the idea of being unloved at the idea of being rejected is why plastic surgery is in style

#dear self: its ok 2 want to b "wifed up" it does not challenge ur idea of women-ism. there is still strength in the wanting of these things

#dear bikram: u make it hard 4winter but real easy 4my summer look. 107 degrees of yes amen oh lord dear lord & namaste

#dear unfit mothers: we 2 r responsible 4 the children we bring onto this earth ur behavior n the world always leaves a breadcrumbtrail home

#dear deadbeat dads: the cycle is only cyclical when you let go of the handlebars

#dear stone thrower: ur glass house be on fire.

#dear self: happy is not a place that you visit on occasion. its a place you should live, often.

#dear love: u feel like home. this is the reason I fear the threat of your daunting kiss.

#dear self: when poetry becomes too much—discover ur smile in things that feel as pretty as the words themselves. Like lemon cake. Ummm

#dear woman: don't wait for him to write you a poem—write it for yourself.

#dear he: today i will post more amazingness from women writers and thinkers. pro-woman doesn't mean anti-man. thank you for staying awhile.

#dear dearest: the truth about love is it feels great when u have even the smallest glimpse but it b amazing when u r loved like u deserve.

#dear love: crawl inside, call it home.

#dear self: when they ignore u, laugh & silence them w/ results. ur a black woman n american, proving urself is a prerequisite

DEAR POET:

THE WIND CAN'T WRITE *itself*

#dear you: u b exactly how god made u. whoever ur god be–u b perfect. When u doubt this most ur shadow should remind u of ur greatness.

#dear highschool: some of your students may have graduated academically—but they're still left back socially. le sigh.

#dear passion: how do i swim you into the blood stream of the shiftless body. how's your breathstroke?

#dear barbie: i don't think you ready for this jelly. i be too bootilicious. from a woman in love with her own damn self.

#dear self: do not lie down w/the fleabitten. do not forget ur callng. it is easy 2 remain silent. speak 4 those unable 2 forgive themselves

#dear youngsta: throw your trash down this shared stairway again and imma whoop you myself. brooklyn stand up.

Dear KISS

U WERE THE BEGINNING OF MY VERY TOUGH FIGHT WITH DISTRUST AND MEN

U WERE ALL THINGS FLYY—TOO. U WERE MY 1ST CRUSH, ALL A GRADE BENEA

THE WALK HOME WITH PLENTY HAND HOLDING. ALL OF THE 2 WEEKS

DONT KNOW MUCH ABOUT PAYING $400 PHONE BILLS. U LIVE

U WERE THE FIRST MISTAKE I WANTED TO FORGET. U KISS

BECUZ OF U I LEARND I WAS ABLE 2 WALK A MILE IN HEE

IT WAS THE SOUND OF UR FIST THAT MADE ME STAND @

I REMEMBR OUR LAST IT WAS B4 I LEFT 4 NYC 4GOOD IT TA

LL OF SUNDAY SWAG. FLAT TOP. JUST FRESH

OF ALL THE THINGS THAT WRITERS DESCRIBE AS MAGIC

. U WERE MY REMINDER THAT THERE ARE GOOD ONES OUT THERE, STILL

BAD IDEA. I COULD SEE THRU THE SLICK KISSING GIMMICK THAT WAS U

ALSO DONE PUTTING ASIDE MY PRIDE. THE CAR RIDE HOME W/OUT U = PERFECT

WAY HIS BODY FLUNG IN2 THE GLASS CAUSING THE WOMEN SCREAMING AROUND US

HE FREEDOM I KNEW U CLD NEVR GIVE ME LIKE THE MAN I KNEW UD NEVER B

#dear world: i mixes ol' dirty & jay-z quotes like batter and chocolate chips. taste good, real good.

#dear twitter: im giving you the expensive shyt for free. you betta recognize.

#dear fear: if got to meet u in a dark shadow anytime in my life. i rather it be over love. i'll go 12 rounds for this thang called love.

#dear world: you ain't neva met a angel like me. and if you do. slap 'em in the mouf for stealing my swag.

#dear fiyah: the day you realize firestarter birthed you, an act of a selfless god, the sooner you will find the peace to burn eternal

#dear firestarter: you be the world's muse. full of noise and beautiful chaos—spin top me a tune in your brightest shade of flame.

#dear truth: u r hard 2 come by. & sometimes, just for good measure—i smacks a chik across the face w/u. loosen teeth, u b egobruise worthy

#dear lemon cake: i will eat you after my show. i will tongue kiss u like a lover should. i will love you lemon cake. like always & forever

#dear woman: today for the remainder of the day i will call u beautiful, just in case. this world makes it so easy to forget.

#dear you: you need a new gimmik.

#dear self: u r made of a bklyn skyline and bay area fog. its ok to bleed, woman. this is no weakness, this is no metaphor—this is ur truth.

#dear women: thx 4 evrything u do. the support &hate. the words of kindness& those of anger. all of it is inspiring. it fits me like a glove

DEAR BLACK:

U BE BEAUTIFUL

#dear tylenol pm: kiss me again.

#dear fingerwaves: i remember wearing you back in 1997.
i think imma bring you back.

#dear universe: bring people into my cypher that are ready
for life bigger than their own ego. supply me with patience,
courage and strength

#dear young world: u can be everything ur parents couldn't,
don't forsake the sacrifice given for ur very breath. Our
tomorrow depnds on u.

#dear heart: the road be like this somedays, beat thru, no
matter how bumpy, uncertain & winding the road.

#dear self: did u say "u are beautiful" to ur reflection this
morning? Did u hug urself tight? Can't nobody love u like u
can.

#dear friends: know what you need for your happy. dont wait til you're 5 years deep in a relationship with an emotional stranger.

#dear fellas: u need 2 share ur issues more. u arent weak when u share—ur weak when u leave it 2 fester. it takes courage to be vulnerable

#dear single lady: it is wrong to offer advice to a woman when your only intention is to have her as a nightclub mate.

#dear biker shorts: you and me will have a misunderstanding if you find your way into my home. FACT. #backintheday

#dear hi top gumby: i saw a young cat sporting you on the train the other day. you've had your day. stay away. #backintheday

#dear kirsti alley: i dont care if you're fat. im fat. wheres my tv show? you wanna move me—make your fat jiggle while playing a ukelele

DEAR TWITTER: MY FAVORITE POEMS HAVE SERIOUS WORDS LIKE:

PUSSY.
WOMAN. MEN.
LOVE.
FORGIVENESS.
KNEES.
FUK.
BALEEN.

BUT NOT IN THAT ORDER...

#dear TLC: you are the reason a noisy sweatsuit short set was worth my entire burger king cashier paycheck.

#dear self: every girl needs 3 things for certain happiness. One of those things are a flyy pair of shoes.

#dear Brooklyn: I've missed u. Imma put on a pretty dress for u & wait for u @ the window. We goin' out soon. U owe me a date.

#dear she: learn to love ur own flaws before requiring him to love u despite them.

#dear lover: I am attracted to the glow of an attentive hand. The fingers the palms the warmth. My skin is ready 4 such attention 2 detail.

#dear lover: I am enamored by the word enamored. I am moreso enamored by a man with a respect for his actions & the power of his words.

#dear he: the stronger ur character—the sexier u become. Man that respects the human frailty is a mighty man indeed

#dear black man: donny hathaway sang "ill love u more than u'll ever know" like his soul was slipping thru his fingers. i kno that sacrifice

#dear hip hop: fallin' in love with you is as inevitable as the ditzy chick dying first in the scary movie.

#dear child: i love you more than i love my own breath. im honored to call you my own.

#dear wind chimes: u have the best job in the world—u were made for sound. and no one ever belittles u for how u move when the wind blows

#dear heart: keep beating

#dear poet: the greatest gift you have to offer this world is a voice of your own.

#dear love: you are the authority in all things beautiful. the reason i fight, sing, smile, laugh & write without abandon.

#dear new york: don't make a fool of me.

#dear love: i need you to find yourself in the homes of more black women. we r leading w/the higest number of "unlikely to be wed"

#dear Bklyn: there is a bridge in my spine. today she is a traffic jam of doubt, full of bodega wishes & lonely. this is when i miss u most.

#dear poetry: u aren't as respected as ur kin, hip hop. but i luv u like personified metaphors, iambic images & breath. u r necessary.

#dear biters: i used to worry about what you was doing, second hand wearing my swag. but now i see—you just playing dress up

#dear self: Repeat: Anyone that doesn't uplift me is a liability.

#dear self: never forget the kinder he is to u—the better.

#dear Mountain Dew: I'd rather drink crab juice.

#dear Chile: all the prayers in my body are for u.

#dear turkey jerky: you are seldomly celebrated. i will celebrate you. all around my mouth.

#dear self: I love when u make u laugh. U tease the moon when u smile like u do. Its what the night skies are meant for.

#dear poetry: look @ ths wonderful life u've given me. Thx 4 the abundance of luv &words &trust &backholding &culture &amazing folk. Humbled

#dear art: you are some type of wonderful. i promise the results of our labor will always be this sweet.

#dear starbucks white chocolate mocha: you are 350 calories worth of hell yea!

#dear flaw: you make me human and beautiful. thank you

#dear moon: you've got women with your name tattooed under their skin. guide them safely home.

#dear ladies: i am almost certain—the way 2 a man's heart is not thru this stomach or his penis—but his mind. ok, maybe a lil penis too.

#dear you: thank you for being here for me to say, thank you.

#dear reader: you can find your smile in a good book.

#dear romance: you are not a walk across the brooklyn bridge just because—you are a walk across the bridge becuz you are hungry for more.

#dear romance: real romance is bills paid on time.

#dear love: falling w/u on my tongue is a verb, an active image, a sound, a noun.

CHECK MY REACH, YO

DEAR SKY: I HEAR U BE THE LIMIT.

#DEAR TWITTER: THE WRITING IS NEVER DONE. NEITHER

#dear self: forgive yourself. You'll get to the next level of happiness much easier that way.

#dear systa: "light-skinded-ded" is really NOT a word.

#dear Oakland: I understand you are the Blues Mack of the west coast.

#dear you: You make me feel like I can be banana flavored.

#dear Quarter Pound: I will mourn you.

#dear Brooklyn: my grandma ain't feelin' u. U've roughened up her 1st grandchild with the brisk hand of sandpaper

#dear self: the sooner you fall in love with you—the sooner we'll have a world of 'amen' in common

#dear Oakland: I am afraid you've fractured my kin. Give me back their jigsaw edges, I'll try to make them whole again.

#dear artist: we all r a part of something bigger, something that existed before us but we here. We r what 2morrow's been waitin 4

#dear she: u are at ur most divine when u love urself loudly.

#dear night: i will start thinking of you as a lover. come wrap me tight. kiss me slow.

#dear writer: when u second guess yourself, u second guess ur gift. when u second guess ur gift the world becomes an imbalanced bulb.

#dear women rappers: reinventing lil' kim is not reinventing the wheel. it is a phoenix descending; wings torn and in flames.

#dear brooklyn: if you bottled your swag in a jar and sold it—we'd be rich.

#dear world: some of these mothers are broken. we cant blame it all on hip hop.the children are suffering. fix them as soon as you get this.

#dear billie: when you sang of morning and heartache—was it a metaphor for self-sabatoge? does it always feel this way?

#dear self: check ur notebook. there is a post it with instructions on how to breath at times like this. follow the instructions closely.

#dear self: u only accept what u are afraid of admitting u would do to others if given the chance. be better, self. u are all u got.

#dear self: doubt is a weapon of mass distraction.

#dear believer: don't stop believing in me. i'm worth it.
i promise.

#dear heart: keep opening wide. there will finally be
someone worthy. the jigsaw don't last forever. soon there will
be safe. & yes. & home

#dear us: #imattractedto women that listen to their heart. &
men that hold her heart like a champ.

#dear oscar grant: i wrote you a poem. it will never be
enough. i am sorry—you deserved better.

#dear nina: my daughter has ur name. she sings like her
heart has survived troubled water. she's a 12yrold feminist,
this is no coincidence.

DEAR SELF: FIND SLEEP.

FIND WATER.

FIND ARMS.

FIND LOVE.

FIND SELF.

FIND SELF.

FIND PEACE IN SELF.

#dear nina: your swag is truly unfukwitable. the rose garden
and gun story—is a bedtime favorite.

#dear universe: #imattracted to men that sleep at home.
brothers that hold hands. fathers that watch soccer games &
buy ice cream afterwards

#dear nina simone: i too understand the pull and undeniable
bend of being misunderstood.

#dear Brooklyn: you are a cranberry belgian waffle with turkey
sausages and bottomless coffee. i like how you wink at me.

#dear police depts: maybe we can get you some interpersonal
workshops to lessen ur need to neglect the people that you're
meant to protect.

#dear bulldog puppy: i want u. really bad. there is no metaphor
to describe this want. i'll walk u everday. we'll watch top chef
together.

BAD

DEAR TWITTER:

CHEATING IS
BAD BREATH IS
SPILL IS
RUSH LIMBAUGH IS
SARAH PALIN'S SENSE
OF DIRECTION IS

#DEAR TWITTER: THE WRITING IS NEVER DONE. NEITHER IS THE

dear afro: you be big and tough and working my scalp something *vicious*.

#dear NYPD: baton asssault has got to stop. seriously.

#dear moon: i got good friends. they smell like u except better they keep me safe like u they lead me home like u. only they hug me tighter.

#dear morning: you smell like sun. Like coffee. Like classes before voices think of carrying the wind. Like now.

#dear poet: read poems. you might save the world. at the very least you will save yourself.

#dear poem: do me a solid. write yourself this evening. im sleepy.

#dear twitter: i could be ur first twitter rapper. all my bars would be in the count of 140 characters. fee: just pay my baby's braces bill.

dear self: when you find the body with your name inked into its dark spaces, make yourself at home

#dear prose: be still. u got sun rays of promise in the horizon. steadfast—women were built for this journey of wait and sigh and finally

#dear heart: stop breaking. its makes it hard for me to get my work done with all that racket.

#dear lover: I dreamt you cheated on me. That's why I woke up and punched you. I blame ur facebook.

#dear MTV: I'm teaching kids performance techniques in nyc streets. We are the best documentary you've never filmed.

#dear twitter: i shot a gun once. it was almost like making out for the first time. except less messy.

#dear you: if loving you is wrong—then the test is just stupid in the first place.

#dear Philly: you are indeed the city of love. salads w/
employees that curse w/their apologies. I like ur swag.
Honest, I do

#dear justin bieber: ask backstreet boys, jordin sparks and
nsync how this movie ends. plan accordingly.

#dear tiger: i dont care about u or ur cheating/ur image ain't
neva been a friend to me/but ur golf game is unfukwitable/stay
gold pony boy.

#dear woman: barbie is not real. your aspirations to be her
drastically denies your greatness and ability of being an
amazing you.

#dear twitter: i knew drama was a "no" for me—cause id
rather punch someone in the face than fuss. and i'm too old
to be fighting.

#dear twitter: best way to get on my good side? pay me on
time & pay me my worth.

DEAR
DAUGHTER:
        USE
           MY
             BACK
                 AS A
                     STAIR
                         CASE.

    MY BONES AS STILTS.

MY MEMORY AS A REMINDER
    TO BE BETTER THAN ME.

#dear twitter: remember to love everything like this.

#dear twitter: real people dealing in real time don't talk in acronyms. LOL & OMG deserve punches directly to the jugular.

#dear artists: the more we accept less than, the longer we perpetuate the starving artist cycle.

#dear twitter: honesty is the best policy. unless of course you can be killed for it. then, a different approach is worth considering

#dear twitterati: if your magnum opus on these here "network" is to correct other folk's spelling...u have less friends than u thought.

#dear twitter: i watch what people say—if they timeline is full of crap, i just don't follow. i don't try to wash out they mouth

#dear twitter: that's like dating a man w/potential to be better. you don't do it. ain't nobody ask you to Tim Gunn his life!

#dear twitter: thats like dating a big girl, cause she got a cute face & you think you can help her lose weight and make her ARMCANDY #fail

#dear twitter: better yet, its like dating a crazy chick and waiting for her brick throwing email reading facebook threatening self, 2 b cool

#dear twitterati: therefore if u cant deal with all my many typos. if your markazz can't just sit back & giggle w/me. u & i ain't goin get along

Acknowledgements

#dear amari: you are beautiful and the reason i do it all. tomorrow is yours. thank you for being such a brilliant and giving daughter.

#dear J: for soccer and turkey burgers for the new york realness. for everything.

#dear falu: for being my rib. for allowing me to be yours. for making me a godmama. again.

#dear vanessa: for being my rock. for letting me be yours.

#dear april, aricka, adam falkner, jon sands, shanelle, aja-monet, airea, eboni, jeannan, cristin, ken arkind, nile & jamaal st. john, leesah, william and leah evans, emily and geoff kagan-trenchard, evan and dasha kelly— my folk that remind me of what flyy and friend and beauty can be when no one is looking.

#dear penmanship artists: for believing in the art and my vision for us.

#dear nuyorican poets cafe, miguel algarin, daemond arrindell & seattle slam, queen godis, roger bonair agard, robbu q. tefler, mayda del valle, doc foster, monica williams, urban word slam team nyc 2010: kamone, justin, jesica, sean b., jay and ish, michael cirelli & the cave canem family: for the continued support, the love and the honor to be part of such greatness.

#dear world that doubts us: thank you for the energy. we will flourish because of it.

#dear AJ: for believing in this project. for kickstarting it. for making me push it to the next level—you are too flyy.

Name Mahogany L. Browne
Location Brooklyn
Web http://www.mobrowne.
com
Bio I'm using this space to
write letters. Because I write
things. I publish them too. I
read a lot. I love like that.

188   1,450   68
following followers   listed

Tweets   7,188

More Praise for #Dear Twitter:

I nominate Mo Browne as the Inaugural Twitter Poet Laureate!
Her tweets give me LIFE!
@EagleNebula

she tweets for the twits & for those with a twist of genius. 140 characters
to twinkle for every character in the twilight.
@QueenGodIs

#dear @mobrowne: You write the most beautiful letters. #nuffsaid
@matador1015

Your Tweets are like sunrise overlooking serenity and everything tranquil.
Just pure "yes" and "know." Keep 'em coming.
@cerothstein

If you don't follow @mobrowne you're seriously missing out, just do it and
thank me later.
@sujennings

@mobrowne love love loving your tweets. thank you.
@karenilsa

Dear @mobrowne I will take these three lessons and share them with my
daughter. Though she is too young to understand, I will save them 4 her.
@kuiet1storm

#dear world-when you least expected to hear the truth, to be praised
@mobrowne spoke it. when you forgot your voice, @mobrowne lifted hers.
@PonyJones

Dear @mobrowne, I sure do wish I had me a plane ticket. I'd be wherever
you are.
@NikkiBlak

follow @mobrowne on twitter if u want a whole world of awesome.
@diyaj

@mobrowne I showed it to my daughter 2day & she couldn't speak.U r
such a beautiful person 4 my teenage girl 2 admire.
@egiptsangeleyes

Am looking at the proof of @mobrowne's new book - collection of her
#dear Twitter tweets. Admit it. You wants one.
@livingpixel